HOW TO GET YOUR BUSINESS FLYWHEEL SPINNING

HOW TO GET YOUR BUSINESS FLYWHEEL SPINNING

A Process to Scale or Sell Your Closely Held Business

ERIC MICHAEL RIGBY, CPA/PFS

Eric Michael Rigby, CPA/PFS
erigby@therigbygroup.com
https://therigbygroup.com/

How to Get Your Business Flywheel Spinning Eric Michael Rigby, CPA/PFS —1st ed.

CONTENTS

INTRODUCTION

Every business begins with a dream...

You, the entrepreneur, wanted to control your destiny and gain freedom over your life while building wealth for you and your family.

Maybe, like many business owners, you started out working for someone else's business. Frustrated by following someone else's lead, you longed for the day you could call the shots and have agency over your career.

The life of an entrepreneur seemed magical...

You harbored fantasies of leading a team that could run your business for you while you could live the lifestyle you've always wanted to live. You imagined how nice it would be to delegate tedious tasks to others while you focused on the fun and exciting parts of the business. You envisioned building wealth that would allow you to live your ideal lifestyle and take care of those you love. Most of all, you visualized the unique imprint your business could have on the world... This vision may have invigorated you as you worked long and hard to build your business.

But now, months or years later, you're wondering if the dream you started with will ever come true.

The challenges and roadblocks entrepreneurs face are varied. Some may have opened this book thinking, "How do I make my business profitable so I don't lose what I've created?" Others think, "I'm working day and night in my business...how do I stop working in the business and finally act like an owner?" And some may be "victims of their own success." Many business owners have become so successful that their schedules are inundated... With no time to step back and evaluate the big picture, successful business owners often feel like they're missing out on opportunities for further growth.

Too often, I meet entrepreneurs who feel lost—they don't have a team of advisors they trust to give proactive, big-picture financial advice that will push them toward their goals.

In my decades of working as an advisor to business owners, I've developed and refined a process to overcome any business challenge and power a business toward success.

I call it the Flywheel.

This repeatable, never-ending process is a simple mechanism that will drive you to your ultimate business destiny and give you the option to Scale or Sell.

I've seen countless business owners use the Flywheel to achieve the freedom they dreamed of when they started. Whether your ultimate goal is to travel the world while your team runs the business for you, sell the business so you can launch your next venture, or simply scale your business so it can have a bigger impact on the world, you can spin the Flywheel all the way to your vision of success.

But even before you reach your ultimate goal, the Flywheel can revolutionize your life. You'll begin to see bigger profits and more clients while working less, feeling less stress, and stepping into the fulfilling, exciting role of an owner-leader...not an owner-operator.

In this book, I'll share how you can begin implementing the Flywheel in your business today, along with other wisdom I've accumulated over the years from guiding entrepreneurs to success.

If you're dissatisfied with your business, you have two options: keep going with the status quo or take the leap to change.

How much longer can you carry on the way things are?

You deserve to live the dream life you envisioned when you became an entrepreneur.

If you're ready to make the change, I'll be your guide. Turn the page and let's launch your business transformation...

CHAPTER 1

Why Isn't My Financial Team Giving Me The Advice I Want?

Most business owners I meet echo the same frustration: "Why am I not getting proactive advice from my financial team?"

Every day, these business owners encounter new information about what's going on in the world of finance, whether they hear it at the office, from a friend, from a colleague, or on the news.

But the one source they aren't hearing it from is their financial team.

"Shouldn't they be coming to me with suggestions and strategies? Shouldn't they be regularly approaching me to ensure my finances are optimized? Are they paying close attention to my business, or am I just another client to them?"

When you're met with radio silence from your financial team, it can feel like you're not important to them. You hired these professionals to share their expertise with you and leverage it to optimize your business. But your expectations aren't being met. It can feel like no one is at the helm of your financial ship.

You worry that you're missing opportunities due to this lack of attention. Each time a business owner friend says, "Hey, did you hear about this financial tool? It's going to do wonders for my business," you think, "What do his advisors know that mine don't? Why haven't my advisors let me know about this tool? Am I falling behind because my advisors aren't paying attention?"

It feels as though you only get advice from your financial team when you pick up the phone and ask them a question yourself. You wish it were the other way around—that they would come to you with ideas and forward-thinking strategies.

Or worse, maybe when you do give your advisors a call, they're difficult to reach or don't give you the personal attention you'd like. You feel as though you don't have a real relationship with them and that they don't truly know you or your goals.

You think, "If I only had someone who knew about me, my business, my goals, and my values as well as I do. If only I had someone who I could call when I'm in a jam and bounce ideas off of. If only I had someone I could trust with my most valuable financial information..."

Running a business can be a lonely operation. Even if you have great people working on your team, there are some decisions and dilemmas that you can't share with them. You're the leader, and you feel the responsibility to keep your team confident in you and your business. This means that if you're facing struggles in your personal life or contemplating a major change in the business, you often have no one to talk to about it. Even if you have close, trusting relationships with those on your team, they can't provide an objective opinion because they have a stake in your business. Your financial team should be an objective voice. But without real rapport with them, your relationship can feel transactional.

Who is on your financial team?

Your financial team is likely made up of your controller, insurance agent, stockbroker, lawyer, and CPA.

A traditional CPA will generally handle your bookkeeping, monthly accounting, and annual taxes. If you have a good CPA, maybe they'll call you into their office in August or September to plan your taxes for the end of the year. There's nothing wrong with what these CPAs are doing, but their business model is focused on lower-level financial tasks, not big-picture strategy. Their role is not designed to be that of a strategic advisor.

You're likely missing the most important role on your financial team—a virtual CFO. Each of your professionals is handling one aspect of your finances, but not one of them sees the big picture. Many entrepreneurs have separate advisors for their personal and business finances, so these professionals can't coordinate the two hemispheres of your finances.

> It's like the story of the 5 blind men and the elephant. Each blind man is touching one part of the elephant, so none of them can figure out what they're touching. The man touching the elephant's trunk thinks he's touching a hose. The man touching the elephant's leg thinks he's touching a tree. The man touching the elephant's side thinks he's touching a wall. And so on. None of them have the full picture, so none of them can make an accurate assessment. A CFO's role is to be the one standing with you looking at the whole picture, providing you with holistic advice.

It's essential to have a close collaborative relationship with your financial team. Every business owner has highly individualized needs, so ongoing, personal communication with your financial team is the only way to ensure you're getting solutions tailored to your needs and not just blanket solutions that they automatically prescribe to all of their clients.

But when your financial team doesn't truly know you, trying to get highly personalized, forward-thinking advice from them can feel like talking to a wall – like the blind man touching only the elephant's side.

You think, "Is there a better, faster, easier way to do this? Why does this have to be such a battle? Shouldn't getting the financial advice I want be a lot simpler?"

Your current financial team helps you check off boxes.

Your tax return is filed. Check!

Your employees are paid. Check!

You have insurance. Check!

Your financial team feels like a pair of hands that gets tasks done, not an insightful advisor. They can help you buy a stock or sell a stock, but they don't stop to ask,

"What does my client want? Does what my client wants align with what I'm doing for them?"

The basics are completed, but no one has an eye for strategy. Your team gets things done, but they don't look ahead for ways to optimize your finances or question why they're taking the actions they're taking. No one is telling you how to put more money in your pocket by leveraging the rules of the game...

CPA, Fractional CFO, Virtual CFO...What's the Difference?

CPA/Bookkeeper: This person is focused on compliance, both with taxes and with other financial regulations. They're looking backward, preparing reports that give you a view out of the "rearview mirror" of the business. But often, they're not working with you on strategies, looking into the future, trying to help you understand where to go with the business and how to leverage your financial situation to get there.

Fractional CFO: Theoretically, this person is there to look out the "front window" of the car, but you're only getting a fraction of their time. This is usually a solo practitioner who is dividing their time between you and many other companies. You're only getting a piece of them.

A Virtual CFO Team: This is a firm that has created a team of people to help you. You'll have a visionary who is helping with strategy from the financial perspective, showing you how to leverage the financial part of your business to achieve your goals. There's also a team of subject matter experts who are there to help you with implementation–such as managing your cash flow, choosing your 401(k), handling your estate plan, planning to minimize your taxes, and other forward-looking, strategic opportunities. The virtual CFO is acting as a quarterback or coordinator for all of the other members of your financial team, including your financial advisor, your wealth manager, your lawyer, your bookkeeper, etc.

Most business owners feel very strongly about taxes. They feel that they're always bringing ideas to reduce taxes to their financial team—when it should be the other way around.

They wonder, "Why am I giving the government such a large percentage of the money I earn? Isn't there a way to put more money in my pocket and build wealth faster?" They want someone to show them how to make the most of the tax deductions afforded by the tax code, yet their team rarely offers up any new, innovative, creative suggestions.

Every entrepreneur wants to build wealth bigger and faster. They accomplish one goal and then set their sights on the next goal. This forward-thinking mindset is what makes entrepreneurs admirable, but many of them don't have the right financial teams in place to proactively support their vision. Their financial teams are focused on the past: last year's tax returns, last year's bookkeeping... The entrepreneur's mind is in the future: "How do I make tomorrow better than today? How can I grow my business and build my personal wealth? How can I accomplish my next goal, and the next, and the next?"

Yet with no financial expert to look into the future with you, it becomes easy to feel stuck in the mud.

FLYWHEEL BUMPER STICKER

Get proactive advice from your financial team.

CPAs look out the rearview mirror (compliance-focused), and CFOs look at what's coming up ahead (strategy-focused).

Not to use finance as a strategic lever is to miss opportunity.

CHAPTER 2

Busy Business Owner Syndrome

When you're a business owner, there will always be too much to do...

As a business owner, you're wearing many hats, both within the business and outside of it. When you're at the office, you're the leader, constantly under pressure to make dozens of decisions in a day.

You have a team in your business, a good one, but it's not a self-managing company yet. You often have to step in to give instructions, make decisions, and correct mistakes. Rather than being the owner who runs the business from above, you yourself still play multiple roles in the business. You feel that if you delegated these roles to your team, nothing would get done the way you want it to be done.

When you get home, you're responsible to your family—and sometimes, there are as many daily decision-making demands coming from your family as there are from your business. Maybe your son is preparing to attend college and needs your guidance in selecting a school. Maybe your daughter needs you to teach her to drive. Maybe your spouse is planning a family vacation and needs your input.

When you add in the other "outside of the office" obligations of entrepreneurship—attending business events, engaging in your community, and staying up to date with the latest news in your industry—you have little time left over. And if you're like most people, reassessing your tax strategy or evaluating your estate plan aren't at the top of the list of ways you want to spend this time.

Yet all the decisions you know you should be making swirl around in your head: "Should I buy a second house? How much money should I put away for retirement? Could I be deducting more from my taxes? Is my estate plan set up correctly? What happens to my business if something happens to me?"

So, you hire financial professionals to take care of those things while you grapple with your demanding schedule. You hope that these professionals can guide you through each decision and help you formulate a plan while you focus on running your business. But as we covered in the last chapter, these professionals aren't always giving you the results you want. They're task-oriented doers, not big-picture strategists. None of them have a holistic view of your business, your finances, your professional and personal goals.

This means that you're the only person responsible for overseeing all the pieces of your financial strategy. But your "Busy Business Owner Syndrome" means that you don't have time to pay as close attention as you want to your finances and their overall context... Your financial professionals aren't looking at the big picture, and you don't have time to look at the big picture—so no one does.

"I'll get to it later," you think. But later never comes...

The Problem with "Later"

A telltale symptom of busy business owner syndrome: constantly thinking, "I'll get to it later."

Whether you're faced with estate planning, paying taxes, preparing for retirement, or even planning your daughter's wedding, you think "I'll get to it later."

But "later" is a fantasy. "Later" is an imaginary, magical paradise where you wake up one morning and don't have 100 things on your plate to take care of. You're a business owner—that day will never come. You will always have too much to do.

When you have too much to do, the urgent tasks tend to overpower the important tasks. In life, it's easiest to deal with what's in front of you rather than with what's most important.

That's understandable... If you see a fire, you, naturally, want to put it out. But the problem with this approach is that, as a business owner, there's a new fire to put out every day. New "urgent" tasks pop up as soon as you complete one of them. The most important tasks get pushed to "later," the day when all of your urgent tasks are taken care of...and that day that will never come.

You think, "I'll get to it tomorrow." But when you wake up tomorrow morning, it's just another "today." Psychologically, tomorrow never comes because we all live in the present. When someone says, "I'll get to it tomorrow," what they really mean is, "I'm not going to do this today." Each day, the task gets pushed aside as the business owner becomes caught up in the day-to-day problems that rear their heads each morning.

This means that you're never able to get to big-picture, strategic decisions about your long-term future. The irony is that this strategic thinking could help you structure your business and your life in a way that would make the urgent, day-to-day tasks less of a burden while putting more money in your pocket.

The Escape Plan

Although you may feel stuck, there's a way out... It's possible to cure yourself of Busy Business Owner Syndrome. Your escape plan consists of four components:

1. **Getting perspective**

   Running a business can feel like being in the midst of a battle. But a battle can't be won if the general is on the frontlines... You need to be on the hill overlooking the battle, where you're able to see the whole picture clearly and formulate a strategy based on it.

   But sometimes, you don't have time to take a step back and gain perspective. That's where your virtual CFO comes in. While you live your life and run your business, your virtual CFO is standing on the hill above, taking in the bird's eye view. Your virtual CFO can say, "Wait a minute. There's danger ahead. Let's reassess your strategy" or "Look over there… I see a potential opportunity. Let's see whether, and how, it could help you reach your goal." Does this decision fit your current strategy? If it doesn't, what needs to change – the decision or the strategy?

Each time you step away from the business to look at the bird's-eye-view and get clarity with your virtual CFO, it will rejuvenate you and give you the energy and momentum needed to lead your business forward.

2. Leveraging a trusted team

To be able to step away from the business and lead it from above, you'll need to surround yourself with a team you trust. In later chapters, we'll cover how to transition your business from one dependent on you to one that your team can operate independently in your absence.

3. Taking care of yourself and your business

Many businesses focus on taking care of their clients and customers first. But if you want to effectively serve your clients and customers, you need to take time to take care of yourself and your family, as well as your business. If you're burnt out, full of stress, and so busy you can't spend the recreative time with your family they and you need, you won't be at peak performance to help your clients. And if you don't have time to implement strategies that make your business run smoother, your clients' experience may be even more chaotic. Even though it seems counterintuitive, your clients will have a more positive experience if you prioritize your own well-being. If you don't, everyone loses—you, your team, your family, and your clients. The better you keep yourself, the better you help all.

4. **Building and energizing your business's flywheel**
   In the next chapter, we'll introduce the flywheel—the secret weapon to defeat Busy Business Owner Syndrome. Note that the flywheel is not a one-and-done strategy. It's a constant, ever-spinning mechanism to power your business. With your flywheel in place, your business will constantly improve, and every action you take will drive you towards your goals.

An Entrepreneur's Journey

I've always had an entrepreneurial spirit...

I grew up lower-middle class, and I knew at an early age that my family didn't have money. When I played baseball as a kid, I remember noticing that everyone else had cleats while I had tennis shoes because my family couldn't afford cleats. From the time I was in 2nd grade, I had a job to earn extra money—my first was delivering papers. I grew up knowing that if I wanted something, I would have to work for it.

After college, I began working at Ernst & Young as a junior accountant and became bored with it very quickly.

I struggled being a public accountant. I did not like sitting in a conference room or at a desk for sixteen hours a day doing what I believed was rudimentary, repetitive analytical work that was not really thought-provoking. I wasn't growing, and I needed that.

And my true desire was to help people... So I quit my job as an accountant.

Right before I got married, I told my wife that I quit my job. She said, "We're getting married in six months...What do you mean you don't have a job?" But I had faith it would all work out.

I talked a business owner into hiring me part-time so I could have a steady stream of income while I started a firm.

Over two or three decades, I built my firm and realized that at its core, my job was about helping people solve problems. I became more of an advisor than an accountant.

Most accountants' favorite word is "no." But my favorite phrase is, "Tell me more about why that's important to you."

Anyone can churn out a financial plan with a piece of software. But I believe people deserve more... People deserve an advisor who will understand their core motivations and develop a holistic solution to their problems and concerns, custom-designed to factor in every aspect of their personal and professional lives.

I made this belief the heart of my business, and over time, as I worked with more clients and gained more experience, I built the processes that you'll read about in this book.

FLYWHEEL BUMPER STICKER

Get a strategic "thinking partner" to ask questions that keep you focused on strategic moves, and keep you out of "firefighting." A virtual CFO is already an expert at this.

The most important strategic move is to identify, fix, and expand your flywheel.

CHAPTER 3

Create Your Flywheel

The flywheel represents how your business should be running in a perfect world. It's a strategy to help make you and your business better at the same time. It's made up of five components:

- Vision
- Culture
- Strategy
- Implementation
- Accountability

As the flywheel spins, it builds momentum. With each rotation, your business becomes stronger, and you eventually build so much momentum that growth seems to happen organically.

The flywheel helps you continually improve your business. "Do I have the right people in the right positions? Should the business be a partnership? An S-Corp? Is now the right time to invest?" The flywheel gives you a concrete process for making big decisions such as these and seamlessly implementing them.

Once you build your flywheel, you have to constantly push it to keep it moving. It won't work if you let it sit idle. And the flywheel is not permanent once you build it... It is a mechanism to execute a plan. If you find that your initial plan has changed, you have to adjust the flywheel so that it's built toward executing your new plan. For example, an engineering firm has a goal of onboarding four new engineers. Once they accomplish this goal, they can't stagnate and still remain productive toward further growth. It's time to move on to the next goal. Now that the four engineers are installed in the business, what's the next most important goal? What decisions, what ideas, would have the greatest impact on the business? When you decide what that goal is, you must adjust the flywheel to support your new goal.

Over time, you have to constantly reassess how the flywheel is working and make changes to it. As the conditions of the market change, you'll reevaluate your plan and adapt it to the present moment, and your next set of goals.

Your flywheel gives you a way to beta-test ideas. If you wanted to fly a plane, you wouldn't just jump in the cockpit and take off—you would learn how to fly first. Likewise, when you get a new idea for your business, you shouldn't rush to implement it without looking at the flywheel and ensuring it fits with your overall vision.

Scale or Sell

Whether you want to scale your business or sell it, the flywheel helps you accomplish that goal.

The flywheel is designed to build momentum that makes scaling your business easy. With each rotation of your flywheel, your business grows and grows. If you want to, you can ride the flywheel for years, putting more money in your pocket and achieving a vision that lives up to your most important values. But if you're looking to exit your business, whether to retire or to pursue other ventures, the flywheel places you in a great position to sell.

It's much easier to sell a business if it's a well-oiled machine that has processes and procedures in place and runs itself without the owner's hands-on daily involvement. If your business is too dependent on you, it's a more difficult sale. Buyers may fear that the business will fall apart if you do not actively participate.

In the current marketplace, it's easier to sell a bigger business than a smaller one, and selling a bigger business will yield you a bigger payday.

If you have 65 restaurants instead of 5, you can net a higher profit selling them—and sometimes it's just as easy to run

65 restaurants instead of 5 because you have the same processes, culture, and vision in place.

The Freedom You've Always Wanted

Further, the flywheel allows you to transition from a "you do it all" business to a team-led business.

It facilitates independence in your team members. You may know the old saying, "Give a man a fish, and you feed him for a day. Teach a man to fish, and you feed him for life." Rather than stepping in to solve problems for your team, teach them how to solve the problems themselves.

Rather than your team relying on you to solve every problem, the flywheel will empower them to solve problems on their own, freeing your schedule to focus on other things. Teaching your team to be independent problem solvers will have a great impact on them as people, too. You are helping them grow. Wouldn't you rather be a business owner who inspires your team to grow, embrace challenges, and push themselves to become better employees – and better people – than a business owner who is content to give people a paycheck just for showing up and performing at the same level year after year? Wouldn't your business be a better place to work – for your team and for you, too - and more attractive to buyers if you're the former?

Finally, you can stop being an owner who works "in" the business and start being an owner who works "on" the business. You embrace your role as the leader, who is responsible for crafting the vision, not the doer, who executes the vision down to the smallest, most tedious tasks.

With your flywheel, you'll no longer be a "firefighter"—the stressed-out business owner running around putting out fires, consumed by the chaos of the urgent, day-to-day tasks. Instead, you can be the calm pilot who knows where you're going and how to get there. While others execute the day-to-day tasks, your role shifts to looking at the business from a high overview level and guiding its vision and strategy. You'll spend more time thinking about the business than working in it. You'll likely find that when you shift to this role, your business will become more successful because it finally has someone at the top devoting their time and energy to strategy. And, since influence comes from the top, your team will become calmer and more confident as they put out the fires themselves.

This shift in your role makes life as a business owner much more enjoyable... It allows you to reap the benefits of your success and focus on what's important—making memories with your family, having new adventures, and seeing what life has to offer beyond the walls of your office. Imagine knowing that your business could be running successfully without you while you're sitting on a beach with your spouse and kids. Scaling your business so it runs independently of you gives you immense freedom—how would you spend your time if you didn't have to work all day every day to keep the business in motion?

One of my clients is a successful lawyer—but he had to work so much that he was rarely home, and his wife was frustrated. She confided in me that she was upset because their only son was about to go off to college, but her husband was so busy with his law career that the three of them wouldn't get much time together as a family before the son left home.

I had already worked with him on his flywheel and helped him reorganize the law firm so it wasn't dependent on him to bring in business. As his time was freed up more and more, he began going to his son's soccer practices, something he would never had time to do before.

His wife wanted to take a family vacation to Europe in the weeks before his son departed for college. "I just don't have time for a vacation," my client told me. He hadn't taken one in years. Though the flywheel had freed up his time, he was struggling to let go of the mindset that he needed to work all the time for his law firm to be successful. I spoke gently to him, "When will you get the opportunity to take a vacation with your family like this again in your life? This is the last summer your son is living at home... This is a big moment for your family... I have a feeling if you don't go you'll regret it for a long time." He took my advice and went on the trip. When he was in Europe, he called me. "Thank you for telling me to go on this trip," he said, "This is one of the best decisions I've made in my entire life."

Sharing important moments with your family is what life is truly about. If your business gets in the way of that, there's something wrong — and it's my mission to help you fix it.

FLYWHEEL BUMPER STICKER

5 Stages of Your Flywheel: The flywheel has five components: Vision, Culture, Strategy, Implementation, and Accountability.

You need to build your flywheel whether you want to sell your business or scale it and keep it.

The flywheel encourages independence in your team members–giving you time and the freedom to use it as you choose.

CHAPTER 4

The Constant Flywheel Improvement Process

Most business owners complain that they need to work "on the business" not "in the business," yet they rarely have time to work "on" the business. The urgent, day-to-day tasks monopolize their time, so they feel they can never take a step back and work on the business at a high level. It can start to feel like they're playing whack-a-mole...

There's never a moment where every problem is taken care of and every task is completed. As a result, the owner can never "zoom out" and work on the business with an eye to long-term strategy.

But with the process of getting and keeping the flywheel moving, it becomes possible to seamlessly work "on" the business regularly and transition away from being an owner who has to work in the business every day to an owner who has the freedom to scale or sell at will, knowing that the business will run itself.

The 5-Stage Cycle

The 5 stage cycle is Vision > Culture > Strategy > Implementation > Accountability. You move through the flywheel in that order. First, you get clarity on what your vision is, then you build a culture that supports that vision, then you come up with a strategy to achieve that vision, then you implement that strategy. Your virtual CFO is there every step of the way to check in regularly and hold you accountable to your vision – and your implementation.

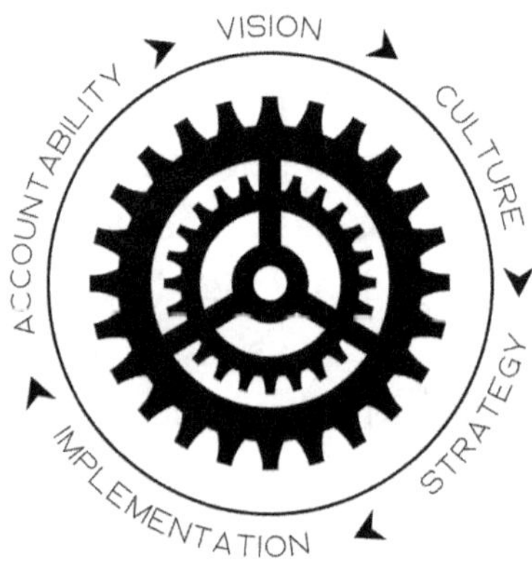

Vision (or The Dream) is where you're headed and why you want to get there. In a perfect world, what does your business look like? What do you want to accomplish with it? At the end of your career, what achievements do you want to look back on and be proud of? What impact do you want your business to have on the world? And for all of these dreams...why do you want what you want? I love to get to know my clients on a deep level and truly understand their desires and what drives them. Uncovering the "why" behind your business can be empowering in many, many ways—and you may not have thought about it before, even though you know the answer deep down.

Sometimes, without realizing it, our ambitions have been shaped by our most formative experiences. A business owner may be driven to become financially successful by the childhood experience of watching their parents struggle to put food on the table. They may be motivated by the desire to build a brighter future for their children or help their parents have a comfortable retirement. Getting to the "why" behind your vision fills you with energy. Your goals become bigger than the boxes you have to check to make money and scale a business. Your goals become about fulfilling your most personal wishes for your life.

Culture represents the values you live by, which attract people to your business – both as clients and as team members. You're more than just a law or engineering firm. What is your higher purpose? What values do you hold dear that you want to transmit to the world through your business? People will only work for money up to a certain point. You need to provide your team with a reason to work for you, a mission to stand behind and champion. If you're a law firm, maybe your mission is to help injured people get back on their feet and receive financial reparations for the damage they suffered. If you're an engineering firm, maybe your mission is to minimize environmental damage by using alternative energy in your projects. Both of these missions are rooted in making the world a better place, not merely making money. Having a mission such as this unites your team and gives them a higher purpose to drive toward and to energize them. And it attracts – intuitively – those who share those values to bring their business to you, rather than going elsewhere.

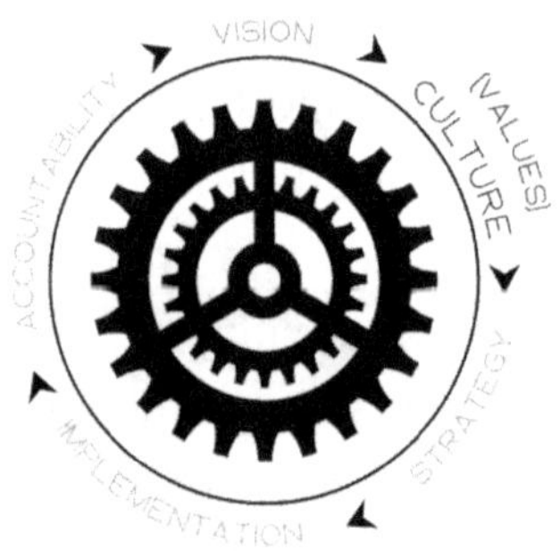

Strategy is your roadmap for making your vision real. It's a plan that is aligned with your vision and culture but also gives pragmatic steps to take to bring these about. Now that you've assessed what you want to deliver, how will you deliver it? What is the smartest, fastest, and easiest way to get to our desired destination?

Implementation (or The Engine) comprises the actions you take toward following that roadmap. Step by step, what needs to be done to make your vision a reality? Who will implement them? Implementation can be broken down into annual, quarterly, monthly, weekly, and even daily steps, and by team member, from yourself to the temporary workers brought in for a push.

Accountability (or The Check-In) is having someone monitor your actions to determine if they're fulfilling your vision. Every month or quarter, we look at your flywheel and assess where you are. "Here's what we said we wanted to accomplish last month. Here's what we actually accomplished last month. What do we need to do next to accomplish your goals? What direction do we need to move in? Does our strategy still make sense? How can we make implementation smoother?" If your goal was to have three junior brokers by the end of the fourth quarter, but you were only able to hire two, your virtual CFO will remind you of your initial goal, help you assess what stood in the way of this goal getting accomplished, and craft a plan to either achieve the original goal or rethink it. "Here's your goal. This is what you wanted. You committed to this, but you're not quite there. What do we need to do to change?"

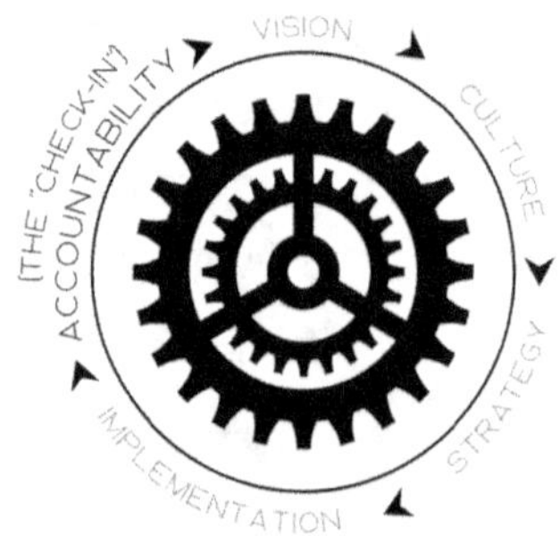

Cycle Up and Repeat

The flywheel is a continuous cycle. After you move through each stage once, you'll begin another loop. "Okay, we've gone through the flywheel, implemented our strategy, and had an accountability check-in. Round two: let's reassess the vision. How do we want to fine-tune your vision, and the process of getting there, this time around?"

Because the flywheel is continuous, your virtual CFO sees you as a client for life and has a true investment in you and your business. While other financial professionals are done rooting for you the second you complete a transaction, a virtual CFO has a stake in seeing you achieve your vision and your ultimate goals.

You can cycle through the flywheel again and again and again, each time with more money, a stronger business and team, more resources, a greater ability to make an impact on the world, more time, more freedom, and a greater enjoyment of life.

FLYWHEEL BUMPER STICKER

Avoid the "Whack-a-Mole" problem: Use the Flywheel to shift from hair-on-fire urgent in-the-business focus to a strategic, leveraged on-the-business focus.

5-Stage Flywheel Cycle: Vision > Culture > Strategy > Implementation > Accountability

Vision: Understand the deeper "why" behind your goals, fueling your energy and motivation.

Culture: Define the values and higher purpose that attract and unite your team.

Strategy: Develop a practical plan aligned with your vision and culture.

Implementation (The Engine): Break down your strategy into actionable steps.

Accountability (The Check-In): Regularly assess progress and adjust as needed.

CHAPTER 5

Getting Clarity

Transforming your business begins with clarity. Before we can formulate a plan, you need to answer two questions:

1. Why is money important to you?
2. Why is your business important to you?

Without the answers to these two questions, the process of scaling a business misses the human element. As business owners, we all love making money, but if making money becomes an end in itself, it becomes easy to lose sight of what's important in life. Answering these two questions will fuel your journey to scaling your business with passion.

When I sit down with a client to talk about these questions, I usually ask "Why?" and keep asking until the client gets to the heart of what's important to them. Maybe the client's first answer to "Why is money important to you?" is "Because it allows me to support my family." My next question would be, "Why is supporting your family important to you?"

With each answer, I'll keep asking "why" until we reach deeper and deeper levels of what is most important to the client. By the end of the conversation, we might uncover the root of the client's relationship with money: "When I was a little boy, my parents were always fighting about money, and it eventually led them to get a divorce. One time, my mom took us to get ice cream, and her credit card was declined, and I could tell she was embarrassed. Even though I was young, I knew this meant we were in financial trouble... I guess I decided to go to business school because I was afraid of ending up in that situation and wanted to build a more comfortable life for my own family."

To this client, money is not just a payout or a bank balance. It's a tool to build a life for his family. Throughout the process of building his flywheel, this client will now have the clarity that his business exists to fulfill his lifelong desire to create a comfortable life for his family. As his virtual CFO, having this conversation helps me understand his motivations at a deeper level and guide him to make decisions that will lead him to what he ultimately wants, beyond just making money or growing his business.

When we have clarity on what drives you, we'll also explore the following questions:

- What are your strengths?
- What are your weaknesses?
- Where have you been?
- Where are you headed now?
- Where do you want to go?
- How are these three answers different—in other words, how do you want your future to differ from your past and your present?

- What are you afraid of?
- What are you looking forward to?

When thinking about these questions, it's important to embrace your past and not run from it. Your past, even if it was full of mistakes and failures, taught you important lessons that helped you get where you are today.

After two or three deep conversations reflecting on these questions, I usually have enough of an understanding of someone's core motivations and values to help them put together a plan. But the process of getting to know a client doesn't end there. Over the entire working relationship, I'm constantly seeking to gain further clarity on who the client is and what they want in life.

I also ask myself these questions, and I encourage you to do the same. Regular examination of all of this is essential for remembering why you're doing what you're doing and why you want what you want. Sometimes, you may find that your initial answers were just scratching the surface of deeper wants and needs. Many people suppress how they truly feel—or sometimes, simply haven't devoted enough time to thinking about it to get a clear answer. Making the time to contemplate these questions will ensure that our plan for "what" to do aligns with your "why."

When we get to the core of what's important to you, our plan to transform your business becomes authentic, and we ensure that we're doing this for the reasons you want to do it, not just basing our decisions on what someone else expects of you. Most people are shaped in a significant way by what others expect of them. Maybe a law firm owner went into the field because his father was an attorney and he expected his son to follow in his footsteps. Maybe an engineering firm owner feels pressured to follow the methods of competitors in his industry, though he deep down has other ideas for how he wants to run his business.

I'm a firm believer in marching to the beat of your own drummer. You don't have to run your business the way everyone else is doing it. Throughout history, all of our most important innovations were made by those who stayed true to their authentic selves. There is no "one-size-fits-all" way to successfully run a business. Getting clarity on who you are and what you value will ensure that your business is driven by your vision—not anyone else's.

It may sound cliché, but I've seen firsthand that when people follow their passion and purpose, money and success usually follow. Yet too many business owners try to do this backward, reverse engineering their actions to get the result of money and success before reflecting on what their purpose in life is. Not only does this leave many business owners unfulfilled, but it also makes it more difficult to achieve money and success because the business is missing the "engine" that having clarity about your purpose provides.

After we gain that clarity, our process will be energized because we've uncovered that you're doing something that's important to you and what that "something," at bedrock, is. Making significant changes to your business can be overwhelming, and it can be easy to procrastinate or lose momentum. But when you know the deeper reason that making this change is important to you, it becomes easier to devote your time, energy, and focus to this transformation.

Throughout the process of gaining clarity, your virtual CFO is your thinking partner. There's enormous value in having someone to bounce these big ideas off of. Sometimes, it's difficult to connect the dots of your own thinking, and it's useful to have someone there to ask simple questions: "Why? What does that mean to you? How do you feel about that?" Your virtual CFO is like a mirror to reflect your thinking back to you.

The Implementation Plan

Once we have this clarity, we'll come up with a monthly, quarterly, or annual implementation plan. The implementation plan lays out every action we need to take to accomplish your goals and by which dates each action will be completed. For example, if the goal is to complete your estate plan, we would break that down into parts: e.g., we need a will (or wills, if you're married), we need trusts, we need powers of attorney. We'll set accountability due dates for each step of this plan.

Once a month or once a quarter, we'll review the implementation plan. What has been accomplished and what hasn't? If something hasn't been accomplished, is it still important? If so, do we need to refocus and make it a goal for the next month or quarter?

The implementation gives you a roadmap and provides a way for you to measure progress. It provides hope... If you begin to feel overwhelmed by everything that needs to be accomplished, the implementation plan reminds you that we're going to eat that elephant one bite at a time.

FLYWHEEL BUMPER STICKER

Start with Clarity: Transforming your business begins with clarity about yourself.

Dig Deep: When exploring these questions, keep asking "why" until you reach the heart of what's important to you.

Motivation and Persistence: Clarity about your deeper purpose acts as a wellspring of motivation and persistence throughout the transformation process.

Leverage a Thinking Partner: Your virtual CFO serves as your thinking partner, helping you explore your thoughts, motivations, and goals.

CHAPTER 6

The Financial Flywheel

Your financial flywheel exists to take you from chaos to clarity. Before you implement a flywheel, it's like you're captaining a ship in rough seas during a hurricane. But after you get your flywheel running, it's like you're sailing effortlessly across a peaceful lake.

You don't want your financial flywheel to be like a twenty-year-old bicycle with a rusty chain. You want it to move effortlessly, so keep it well-oiled, well-maintained, and well-trued.

From Chaos to Clarity

One of our clients is a successful real estate investor who owned about 25 entities—operating companies, a mortgage company, a property company, a finance company, and management company, and multiple trusts. Yet she had struggled with depression since her father's death, and was unable to keep her finances up to date. Before working with me, she had what I call a "Walmart accountant," the type of transactional, sales-oriented professional who offers clients a one-size-fits-all approach without truly getting to know them on a deeper level. This accountant kept telling the client that they would take care of her finances, but they didn't want to clean up the mess. Eventually, the situation progressed to the point where she started to receive IRS notices.

She was referred to me, and in our initial meeting, she opened up to me over several hours. She confided that her mental health problems were making life overwhelming, and she just didn't have the capacity to manage her finances. She was frustrated because her accountant wasn't returning her calls, she didn't feel like she had a relationship with them, and she didn't trust the advice they gave her.

We took her through our process and came up with a plan for each of her entities based on what she wanted for and from them. Her estate tax returns and income tax returns for the estate hadn't been filed, and distributions had been mistakenly made to the heirs prematurely. We brought her accounting up to date for the tax returns and figured out how much income the estate had over a period of years and whether it was interest, dividends, or capital gains income.

We also created a trust for her challenged brother whom she financially supported. We restructured the investments in this trust and appointed a trustee who would ensure the brother would have enough money to live on comfortably each year without being able to make irresponsible decisions with it, which had been an issue in the past. We also ensured that her brother had an estate plan with the correct heirs and that he had the correct beneficiaries stated on his retirement accounts.

This client's finances were a complete and utter mess when we met her. But by getting to know what she wanted and needed, and implementing her own flywheel, we were able to take her from chaos to clarity. This was a great comfort to her during a difficult time and enabled her to focus on getting mentally healthy while knowing her finances were taken care of.

Leveraging Opportunity

Two engineers in their 30s worked for a company, making about $150,000 a year each. They were fed up with their boss, who was constantly absent and didn't provide the company with leadership, forcing the two of them to step in and manage relationships with major clients and make sales while also executing the engineering. Meanwhile, they were making the same salary they had been before, and weren't reaping financial rewards for the additional roles they were taking on.

They came to me for advice, and I had a long discussion with them to find out what their goals were. At the end of our talk, they concluded that what they really wanted was to start their own engineering firm. Though this was what they wanted, they were scared of making this decision—they didn't want pushback from the boss, and they both had young families to support, so they didn't want to go out on a limb only to fail. Yet they knew they had to take this leap... Their day-to-day lives were miserable, they resented their boss, and they didn't feel the hard extra work they were putting in was appreciated. I reassured them that we would put together a step-by-step plan to make this transition as smooth as possible.

We spent three months developing what their cash flow would look like if they had their own business. The banker they went to for a loan initially refused, so I talked to the banker and overcame his objections. I had them quietly reach out to their top clients and ask if they were happy with the work they were doing and if they would be comfortable moving to their new firm. Before doing this, I made sure they didn't have non-compete or non-solicitation agreements and found them a lawyer in case there was pushback. We completed each step along the path to exiting the old firm and establishing the new one. Within two years, they had a several-million-dollar firm with 10 engineers, and we're continuing to refine their flywheel today. For example, our next major goal is implementing project management software.

Without going through this process, these two men may have, out of fear, stayed with their original firm and missed out on leveraging the enormous opportunity before them. The flywheel system isn't just for moving people from a mess to clarity... Sometimes, it's helping people move from relative success and comfort to a bigger opportunity, one more aligned with their vision for their lives. The flywheel is what you need it to be - and what you make of it.

I did something similar for a law firm... Several lawyers were disgruntled because they felt that the senior partners were pocketing most of the profit, while they did most of the work. I sat down with them and said, "Tell me your vision." They told me about their desire to build a new firm together. During the process of launching the firm, a unique opportunity landed in their laps... Their major clients were in insurance, and Hurricane Laura suddenly created a huge surge in the market for their services. We put together a plan to leverage this opportunity, and they were able to grow their business and raise their rates. Now, they're enjoying great success, and most importantly, they're all much happier because they're serving their own vision, not someone else's.

Several months into the pandemic, a potential client who owned a chain of 65 restaurants called me. His "Walmart accountant" had told him not to take a PPP loan, but he didn't trust that advice and took a multi-million dollar PPP loan anyway. Now, his accountant was telling him to give the money back because he didn't deserve it—his chain was primarily a drive-thru, so its ability to make a profit wasn't threatened by the lack of customers dining out during the pandemic.

I looked at the law and the IRS guidance, which said that anyone who believed they could be adversely affected by the pandemic in the future was eligible for the loan. I knew based on our conversations that he had struggled to find meat for his restaurants due to supply chain issues, and according to the guidelines, that was one factor that, among others, helped make him eligible for a loan because it had the potential to cause stress and uncertainty in his business. We were able to get his large PPP loan forgiven without an audit.

I then took a look at his entities. He had about 150 entities to operate his restaurants... Something wasn't right. I helped him clean up the way his business was organized and was able to save him $20 million in 2020. In 2021, he decided to retire and exit the business, and I helped him make that transition. After the sale of the business, I encouraged him to take a few months to take a breath and think about how he wanted to spend the rest of his life and avoid taking risks with his money during that time.

Now that he's retired, I still act as his virtual CFO and coach him through money decisions. Recently, he called me wanting to buy a $600,000 Rolls Royce. I asked him, "Is there anything you could do with that money that would give you more happiness?" He said, "I'm a car guy." After working with this man for years, I knew him well. I knew that money was important to him because he grew up without great resources so he was driven by the desire to show his wealth as a way to celebrate that he'd had success despite his origins. A CPA's favorite word is "No," but a good virtual CFO's favorite word is "Why?" It's not my job to shut him down or get him to make decisions that fit my personal views of wealth and how to handle it. It's my job to understand what he wants to do, and why he wants to do it and help him make that decision in the best way possible. I told him, "You have plenty of money available to make that purchase. If it makes you happy, go for it."

The Components of the Financial Flywheel

To determine if your financial flywheel is working, answer the following questions:

- Is your business as profitable as you want it to be?
- Are you paying more in taxes than you need to?
- Are you able to manage debt and risk effectively?
- Are you taking out as much cash as you'd like?
- How is your business cash flow?

- Do you have someone you trust who can help you think through and solve your financial problems?

The result of the flywheel is confidence. Now that you have everything in place, you can move forward knowing that you have a plan for the future that you're confident in.

FLYWHEEL BUMPER STICKER

Components of the Financial Flywheel: Profitability, tax management/minimization, debt and risk management, and cash flow maximization.

Do you have a trusted advisor looking at strategic deployment and management of your Financial Flywheel?

CHAPTER 7

Full Team Leverage

Imagine that your business could be fully run by your team, without you having to step into the day-to-day operations. While you guide the overarching vision of the business, your team operates the business independently, like a machine. Creating a self-managing company doesn't happen overnight. To enable your team to do this, you need to create systems that they can leverage.

Full team leverage gives you momentum whether you want to scale or sell. It makes your business more attractive to own, more attractive to work for, and more attractive to buy.

If you prefer to remain as the owner, a team-led business gives you a level of freedom you've never had before. Currently, you may be working sixty- or eighty-hour weeks to keep your business running successfully. This level of work leads to stress and burnout and minimizes the time you have to devote to your personal life. But when your team is capable of running the business without you, you can kiss those long, overwhelming hours goodbye. You can minimize your role so that you're only performing tasks that use your unique ability. Your time at work becomes more enjoyable because you're only doing tasks that you love to do and that are easy for you because they tap into your existing expert skillset.

Or maybe you don't want to work in the business at all but want to provide a guiding vision that others execute. You could travel the world with your spouse, spend a morning at a golf course, or attend your kid's soccer game—all while knowing that the business is running smoothly without you. For many business owners, reaching this point in their career can be an emotionally gratifying experience. For years, they made sacrifices and missed out on time with their family while they were building the business. Now, they can enjoy the fruits of their labor, make memories with those they love, and take part in all the activities they pushed to the side while launching their career.

If you want to sell your business, a self-managing company is extremely attractive to buyers. If your business relies totally on you, potential buyers will worry that the business won't be able to remain successful when you're no longer there. When they step in as the new owner, they want the lifestyle freedom offered by an owner-independent business, not the hectic life of an owner who has to work sixty to eighty hours a week "in" the business.

To create a self-managing business, you need to get clarity around roles. What is the role of an owner? What are the roles of key team members? Create an outline of precisely which tasks each team member is responsible for on a monthly, weekly, and daily basis. How can you delineate your team's roles so that the business runs more efficiently? You may find that you need to add team members or hire more experienced or qualified candidates. If you come to this conclusion, does your business model and pricing support hiring additional team members or raising salaries to attract top-performing employees? If it doesn't, our next plan of action is to implement value-based pricing that allows you to increase your fees and afford the team you need.

Value-based pricing means that you set your prices based on the value your customer perceives that they're receiving, not by the hour. For an engineering firm that builds storage facilities and typically bills at $200 an hour, value-based pricing could look like setting a flat rate of $25,000 to engineer a storage facility. Value-based pricing allows you to set a rate that's tied to the value you bring, not the number of hours you work. At the $200 an hour rate, your team would have to work 125 hours to make $25,000. But if your team sets a flat rate and can complete the project in less than 125 hours, you net a higher profit than you would with an hourly model. With that extra profit, you have more room in your budget to get the right people on your team, those who will create leverage for the business to grow and who will increase its value. With that increased budget, you also can create employee benefit plans that can attract and retain top performers. Your virtual CFO can help ensure that you allow the appropriate time frame and length for the project so that your profit grows with value-based pricing – never underestimate.

Scaling your business requires delegation. To give your business momentum, you need to remove low-value tasks from your plate (and those of the key players on your team). One owner I worked with did his own accounting at night. I helped him outsource that role to an accountant who charged

$30 an hour. The cost of hiring this accountant was minimal, and it freed up the owner to spend his time working on the business or simply spend his evenings with his family.

You may also want to explore the option of getting paid upfront rather than billing for work after the fact. When you bill after a project is complete, you're essentially lending your own cash flow to finance the client's project. What happens if something goes wrong and the client delays or cancels the project before you get paid for the work you put in? By asking for even a portion of your payment upfront, you minimize the chances of losing your cash flow to a client. We'll also investigate your billing process. Many businesses still send paper invoices and accept checks. In this day and age, technology exists that enables your clients to safely deposit money to your account online after receiving an invoice via email. This simple adjustment to your process helps you accelerate cash flow and avoid financing your client's work.

Once you define the roles of your business and fill these roles with the right people, you need to ensure you have the systems and processes in place that allow your team to operate on a larger scale. How can you make each role's process more efficient so each team member can leverage their time to get more done? Do you need systems or software to speed up this process?

Each person on your team should document the process they use to complete each of their tasks. With these processes documented, you can analyze and refine them so that they're as efficient as possible. More importantly, documenting your processes means that it's easier to onboard new employees.

For example, if you're scaling from two engineers to five, having those two original engineers document their processes will help the new engineers quickly fit into your business, giving you greater capacity to take on new clients. Documenting these processes also means that you won't have to panic if a key employee leaves because you can easily teach someone to fill the role – it's all laid out and ready for them.

To create a self-managing business, you need to build a strong and efficient financial tracking system. What financial software do you currently use? If you don't have any, it's key to get the right system installed so your business's finances are organized, tracked, and automated. You'll also want to create and test internal controls to create security around cash in the business. I've seen a few horror stories unfold in which trusted employees embezzled money from a company... It's easy to prevent theft of this kind with simple internal controls.

As part of your financial system, we'll implement quarterly financial reviews to ensure your system is running smoothly.

With these systems in place, you can achieve full team leverage–and experience freedom you've never had before.

FLYWHEEL BUMPER STICKER

Full Team Leverage for Business Growth: Creating a self-managing team is essential for business growth and owner freedom.

Clear Roles and Efficient Systems: To achieve full team leverage, define clear roles, hire the right people, implement efficient systems and processes and document them.

Scale or Sell: A self-managing team is the fundamental ingredient in businesses that are able to scale or that sell for high multiples.

CHAPTER 8

Installing Safety

Though scaling can open the doors to more money, more opportunities, and more freedom, it can sometimes be dangerous... Sometimes, you're in a great position to throttle up and scale faster, and other times, you need to pull back before you go out of control. To prevent chaos, it's helpful to have a virtual CFO by your side who can help you run the throttle.

When you scale, it's easy to get distracted by shiny objects and lose focus on your core business – and your core goals. As you accumulate more money and free time, you may get excited about launching other opportunities beyond your first business. One client successfully scaled a business that performed marketing services for car dealerships. But when the pandemic happened, supply chain issues slowed car manufacturing. Instead of focusing on solving the challenges his first business was facing, he decided - against my advice - to jump into the roofing business. He lost half a million dollars and spent needless hours running a company that eventually closed.

If you're an entrepreneur, it's likely that you have a "jump in and take action" personality. Your willingness to take risks is what enables you to be an entrepreneur, but left unchecked, this personality trait can lead you astray. You may want to jump in and invest as soon as you see a potential opportunity, but without taking a moment to put on the brakes, consider a decision deeply, and go into a new opportunity with a well-thought-out plan of action, you may lose money and give yourself a headache. With a virtual CFO, you have someone always at your side to vet and filter potential opportunities and guide you in your decision-making process. Someone to ensure your risks are thoroughly calculated, and all possibilities taken into account before the leap is made. Each time you get enthusiastic about a new business idea, your virtual CFO is there to say, "Okay, let's take a breath. Does this decision fit your strategy of what you want for the future?"

If only I had a dollar for every time a client told me, "My friend wants me to invest in ___"...

As an entrepreneur, the people in your life will always come to you with new ideas and opportunities. It can be easy to get swept along by someone else's enthusiasm, especially if you have a close personal relationship with that person and don't want to disappoint them. But not every one of these ideas is destined to lead to success... Your virtual CFO is there to act as a guardrail keeping you from leaping into an ill-considered business venture without properly thinking it over.

A client was encouraged by one of his buddies to buy a 2 million dollar farm on which he could take people duck hunting. I helped him come up with a structure and a business plan. He spent $500,000 on equipment for the farm, and I began to realize that he was acting as if this business was a fun leisure project and not an attempt to create a commercially viable business. He got it in his head that he wanted to use the business as a tax deduction. I pulled the throttle... "Why put yourself at risk? You're financially set for the rest of your life... Let's set up the structure of this business correctly before jumping in and deducting it from your taxes."

Bright, sparkly objects can distract you from your efforts to get and keep the flywheel running in your core business. There are infinite opportunities out there, and you could waste a lot of time seeking them out, all while taking your eye off your core business. Your virtual CFO will help you avoid self-sabotage and keep you steady on the path to your goals.

To keep entrepreneurs from getting distracted by mere shiny objects, we'll remain focused on their quarterly and annual plans until the flywheel for their core business is working smoothly for a few cycles. Some new business opportunities may support your flywheel for your core business. For example, vertical integrations such as owning your office building can support your core business by helping you build equity in that building. This opportunity may be a smart decision, whereas trying to launch a second business in an industry you have no experience in would jeopardize and distract you from your plan to scale your core business. Your virtual CFO will be an essential resource to differentiate between useful opportunities and "shiny objects."

But – let me say it again – your virtual CFO's job isn't just to say "no" to you. It's about thoroughly evaluating each opportunity and determining which ones have a legitimate place in your plan and which ones are just distractions from your goals.

FLYWHEEL BUMPER STICKER

Avoid Shiny Object Syndrome: Scaling a business can be exciting, but it's essential to stay focused on your core business.

Prevent Financial Risks: It can be tempting to use new ventures as tax deductions or investment opportunities without proper planning. A virtual CFO can help structure these initiatives correctly, minimizing financial risks and ensuring they contribute positively to your overall strategy.

Balanced Evaluation: Your virtual CFO's role isn't necessarily to say "no" to new ideas but, rather, to thoroughly evaluate each opportunity based on its potential to support your overall plan. They will assist you in making informed decisions that align with your business goals.

CHAPTER 9

Your Life and the Flywheel

Before your virtual CFO can understand your business, they have to understand you, the entrepreneur behind it. How does the business facilitate your personal goals?

This begins with understanding why money is important to you.

When I first meet with a client, I start by asking them to tell me about their current financial reality. "I have this amount of money in my brokerage account, this amount of cash, this amount saved for retirement. I have two houses." I get an overall picture of their financial situation. Then, I dig deep into the question "Why is money important to you?"

One version of this conversation might go something like this:

"Why is money important to you?"

"I need to provide for my spouse and kids."

"Why is that important to you?"

"I have four kids. I love them, and I want to make sure I can get them through college."

"Why is that important to you?"

"I had to pay my way through college, and I graduated with debt. That made my life difficult, and I don't want my kids to have to suffer like that."

"What do you mean by "suffer"?"

"Well, I used to hear my parents fight all the time about money, and I didn't want to be a burden to them. So I went out and borrowed money to go to college, and I didn't tell them because I didn't want to add to the burdens they were already carrying."

"What was it like when your parents fought about money?"

"It caused chaos and conflict. I was always scared to ask for money. I only had one pair of shoes, and I was embarrassed by them. I always wanted Nikes growing up, but I knew my parents couldn't afford that. I don't want my kids to feel the same way about money..."

During this conversation, I gain an understanding of the root of why money is important to this entrepreneur. Then, I can better devise and facilitate an individual program and strategy for his finances and his business.

The Business is Your Benefactor

As an entrepreneur, the business is your benefactor. It exists to provide you with the life you want—not the other way around.

To make the business your benefactor, you need to know what you want out of life beyond the business.

You can grow your business as much as you want, but if you're working 100 hours a week, what's the point?

Your business is just a means to an end: the life you want. Your business enables you to do things like send your kids to college, take your family to the Bahamas, buy football season tickets… whatever sparks joy in your life.

Your business is also a benefactor to your employees. As you grow your business, you're also helping your team achieve their own personal and financial goals. You're providing them with a means to support their families and achieve their dreams in the same way that you are.

Just as you run your business in a way that supports your personal life, your business should support the personal lives of the team members who work for it. If one of your employees is a mother with four kids, maybe you adapt your workplace policies to allow her to pick up her kids from school. You and your employees should share an understanding that, though the business is important and everyone should be held to a high standard, your family and your values are what's truly important in life.

As an entrepreneur, your business is a means to live in alignment with your values. One client owned a real estate company she inherited from her father. Her father was charging 20% in a 3% market, which was perhaps, in the short-term, a savvy business move, but was taking advantage of people who were in a tough situation. My client felt guilty about this practice, and it created great conflict within her. I told her, "If it makes you uncomfortable, don't do it. We can refinance it. Your business practices have to be aligned with your values, or you'll drive yourself crazy." If you contradict your values, you won't feel good about yourself, and your choices will weigh on you.

What are the core values of the company? Why does it exist? What are you and your team trying to do? You have to share the answers to these questions with your team. People work for much more than money. They work for people they like, people they trust, people that they think are trying to do good in this world. When your employees believe in the mission and values of the business, you'll have engaged, committed and genuinely motivated team members who will give your flywheel more momentum.

Because you're an entrepreneur, your business finances and your personal finances are married. You own the assets on both sides of the equation. Every decision you make in your personal life impacts the business and every decision you make in the business impacts your personal life.

If you don't take care of your business's financial flywheel, you can create havoc in your personal life. Conversely, if you make poor decisions with your personal finances, you can fall short of your business goals.

Because your business and personal finances are intertwined, your virtual CFO is more than just a CFO—they are your personal financial confidant as well.

FLYWHEEL BUMPER STICKER

The Business is Your Benefactor: Your business should serve as a means to an end, not the other way around. It exists to provide you with the life you desire. Define what you want beyond the business to ensure the business supports your personal goals.

CHAPTER 10

Scale or Sell

Now that the flywheel is running efficiently...what do you want to do next?

You've built a business that's both a dream to own and a dream to sell. You have a solid choice either way, so now it comes down to determining the right decision for you at this time in your life. You're at a fork in the road and have two exciting paths you could go down. Where are you on your journey? What's important to you at this moment in your life? What will the next phase of your life look like? Do you want to build to scale or build to sell?

This decision can take weeks or months of reflection to get clarity on. It comes down to knowing what you want your experience of life to be like.

Here are some questions to consider:

- Do you enjoy your business? Does it spark joy? Do you like what you do?

- Do you have the desire, the energy, and the enthusiasm to grow your business to the next level that you desire? Are you committed to scaling the company?
- How long do you want to continue working?
- Where are you in life? What's important to you?
- How do you want to spend the next two or three years?
- What's the best decision for you, your family, your employees, and your business?

If you're full of passion and energy, and you have the desire to continue working, then scale. But if you're burnt out and ready for a change of pace, you may prefer to sell.

Recently, I met a doctor in his sixties whose career clearly sparked joy in his life. You could see in his eyes that he loved to talk to patients. I asked him, "How long do you want to work?" He said, "As long as my eyes and hands work." He told me that he had enough money that he could retire today, but that he gets joy from helping people.

On the other hand, I knew a law firm owner who was completely and utterly burnt out. He enjoyed his challenging career when he was younger, but he was now craving a change of pace. "I've given so many hours of my life to my career," he said, "I've accomplished what I wanted to accomplish—now I want to give my hours to my family."

I'm a true believer in the clichéd saying "Love what you do and do what you love" (most clichés become those because they're so often true). If you love running your business, devoting yourself to scaling will be an exciting endeavor. But if you recognize deep down that you no longer love what you do and would rather spend your time elsewhere, it's time to prepare for your next chapter and sell the business.

Build to Scale (and Hold)

If you decide to scale and hold onto your business, you're going to move toward what I call the "Warren Buffet Model." Warren Buffet doesn't work "in" any of his businesses... His businesses work for him and generate a large profit. Buffet has said that he spends most of his time sitting in his office reading, deepening his knowledge of business, and staying up-to-date on the latest financial news while his businesses run independently of him. He doesn't have to worry about overseeing the daily operations of his businesses and can instead research potential opportunities and refine his existing businesses.

A key component of the scaling process is gradually releasing yourself from working "in" the business and delegating "in" the business work to your team. When you begin the scaling process, you may have started with delegating low-level tasks such as bookkeeping. But as your business grows, you're able to delegate increasingly important tasks and free up more of your time to work "on" the business. Eventually, you can implement a professional management team so that you don't have to work "in" the business at all. You're at the top of the pyramid, and are needed only to make the most crucial, big-picture decisions about the business.

If you own a restaurant chain, you can't be the guy flipping hamburgers... You need to be several levels above so that you have enough perspective to make decisions about the direction of the business. While others operate the business, handle accounting, train employees, and execute marketing strategies, you're able to focus on decisions like, "We have an opportunity to open a restaurant in a town where we don't currently have one. Can we afford to buy the land? Will our restaurant appeal to the demographics of the location? Do we have a management team who can run the restaurant? Does this fit with our long-term strategies for the business?" If you're busy working "in" the business, you wouldn't have the time or perspective to notice and evaluate this opportunity. When you do decide on your plans for the new restaurant, you delegate the execution of your plan to your team, while you continue to enjoy your life and cash in on your business.

When you reach the pinnacle of scaling, you become an owner, period, not an owner-operator. You guide the business's vision, strategy, and culture, but others execute your ideas for you. You can live your life while the business acts as a machine generating a profit for you... You're the Warren Buffett of your company!

Build to Sell

If you decide to sell your business, it's crucial to determine a plan for what's next. Entrepreneurs are active, energetic people, full of passion and ideas. If you jump from a stimulating, thrilling life of running your business into a relaxing, calm retirement, you may become bored and restless. What do you want to do with the rest of your life? Maybe you want to exit your current business so you can launch a new business idea. Maybe you want to turn your attention to philanthropy and make an impact in your community. Maybe you want to accomplish a goal you've always had in your mind, such as writing a book, training to run a marathon, or planning a cross-country road trip with your spouse.

Everyone, especially those with an entrepreneurial mindset, needs a purpose, so before selling your business, you need to take some time to consider what your purpose will be when you're no longer focused on scaling your business. What do you want your future to look like?

If you sell your business, will the financial outcome fund the rest of your life? If it won't, do you plan to launch another business or leverage your expertise in another way? It's important to have a plan for your next venture in place before letting go of your first business.

I recommend that entrepreneurs take 6-12 months off after the sale of their business. Your entrepreneurial "let's jump in and start" mindset might drive you to begin another business as soon as your first business is out of your hands. But this is an enormous transition in your life, so you need to take a step back and get clarity on the direction of your life before committing to another business too quickly. You may launch a new business in that first year only to find that it was a rash decision made because you didn't know what to do with yourself after exiting your business.

Finding the right buyer

So you've decided to sell your business... Now, it's time to find the right buyer—not just any buyer. With your virtual CFO, you'll reflect on what's important to you with this sale. What terms are you looking for? What is your goal for this sale? What qualities and goals will the right buyer need to ensure that this sale accomplishes your goals?

Sometimes, you may not be able to find the right buyer right away. Rather than settling for less, you may decide to stay in your business and scale for another year or two so that you're in a more favorable position to find the right buyer.

The decision to scale or sell isn't a permanent one—these are simply two directions you can move in. It's possible to change directions so that you can achieve the big-picture outcome you're looking for.

CONCLUSION

The choice is yours...

You could put this book down, wake up tomorrow, and continue to run your business the way you've always done it. You can continue to feel "stuck" in your current challenges... And continue to long for a different lifestyle, one where you have the ultimate freedom to run your business rather than being run by it.

It's tempting to stay in your comfort zone... But how "comfortable" is it, really?

No one can take the leap for you. It's up to you to put down this book and take the next step toward your dream future.

Take a moment to imagine what that future looks like...

For some, this could mean becoming a "Warren Buffet" style owner who doesn't work a day in the business but collects a large check when the business profits. With this free time and financial success, your options are unlimited... You could spend a year traveling the country – or the world - with your spouse while the money keeps rolling in. You could spend your time pursuing other ventures such as becoming a thought leader in your industry or launching a charitable venture. When you win back your time, the paths of life open up before you and become yours for the taking.

For others, implementing the flywheel can get your business in shape so it can be sold. Maybe you're nearing retirement age and want to sell your business so you and your spouse can live your retirement fantasy. Or maybe you're earlier in your career and want to sell your current business so you can launch your next business—and build your entrepreneurial empire.

No matter what your ultimate goal is, the flywheel can set you on a path toward it.

But from the moment you implement the flywheel, you'll feel its impact. Running your business will become easier, more pleasurable, and more profitable. There's a satisfaction that comes from knowing you're on the right track, and you'll no longer feel stuck.

If you want to implement the flywheel in your business, you have two options: you can do it yourself or hire a virtual CFO to guide you through the process, help you achieve and maintain clarity, and hold you accountable – to your deepest goals.

Some entrepreneurs may feel motivated to implement the flywheel themselves, but a word of caution... When you're in the trenches of running your business, it can be difficult to get an outside, objective view. It's like flying a plane with no air traffic controller. At times, you may get bogged down in the day-to-day insanity of running your business and fail to spot opportunities and challenges ahead. A guide can remove the pressure from you as the owner and become a trusted voice that helps you achieve your ultimate goal.

NEXT STEPS

For the right business owner – someone who isn't satisfied with the status quo, who has a bigger vision for his or her business, and is ready to scale the business and shift from "in-the-business" operator to "on-the-business" owner, or who is ready to prepare the business to sell – Rigby Financial Group's Virtual CFO program may be the catalyst for growth you've been looking for.

Get hours back into your day by offloading your financial tasks.

Get a Personal Virtual CFO who:

- Listens first, knowing your goals are unique, and develops a holistic plan with you.
- Understands your complete business and personal financial matters at all times and makes you a priority.
- Communicates with you often with outreach, regularly scheduled updates, meetings, and unlimited emails and phone calls as the need arises.

Here's how we can help your business thrive:

Financial Services – You don't always know what's around the corner, so we'll help you plan for the unexpected and protect your business and loved ones.

Outsourced Accounting – We help organize your accounts, complete your bookkeeping and payroll, and ensure you are as tax-efficient as possible.

Business Consulting – We work closely with you to understand what challenges are impacting your business so you can make clear, fully informed decisions about how to tackle them.

Strategic Planning – Take charge and plan for the future of your business with forward-thinking strategies to implement.

Equity Management – From stock options to raising capital, we are here to provide answers.

It starts with a 1-hour free consultation where you tell us what you hope to achieve.

Learn more at https://therigbygroup.com/.

ABOUT THE AUTHOR

Eric Michael Rigby has enjoyed running his own business for close to 30 years. He loves getting to know clients on a deep level, which in part accounts for the fact that many of RFG's clients have been with the firm for decades (though Eric loves welcoming new clients he and his team can proactively serve).

Eric takes joy and satisfaction in devising strategic, holistic solutions, and solving problems to improve clients' lives, both professional and personal. Most of his working hours are spent meeting with clients to discover how he can best help them, and then devising the strategic solutions that will provide that help – to ultimately improve every area of their lives.

He is also dedicated to his firm and team, and their shared vision for the future, as well as RFG's firm culture – which encourages every team member to grow and develop both new and existing skills, as well as to enjoy their personal time fully.

Eric lives by what he preaches – his core values of service, teamwork, and making time for both work and the invaluable recreation afforded by time spent with family and friends.

Top 5 Strengths: Futuristic-Arranger-Command-Empathy-Individualization

www.ingramcontent.com/pod-product-compliance
Lightning Source LLC
LaVergne TN
LVHW020049110826
845155LV00029B/697

* 9 7 8 1 9 5 5 2 4 2 9 2 9 *